Saints

Books by Reginald Gibbons

Roofs Voices Roads *(poems)*
The Ruined Motel *(poems)*
Saints *(poems)*

Selected Poems of Luis Cernuda *(translations)*
Guillén on Guillén: The Poetry and the Poet
    (translated with A.L. Geist)

The Poet's Work: 29 Masters of Modern Poetry on
    the Origins and Practice of Their Art *(editor)*
Chicago *(editor)*
Criticism in the University *(edited with Gerald Graff)*
TQ20: Twenty Years of the Best Contemporary
    Writing and Graphics from TriQuarterly Magazine
    (edited with Susan Hahn)
The Writer in Our World *(editor)*

Reginald Gibbons

SAINTS

poems

The National Poetry Series
Selected by Roland Flint

Persea Books
New York

for Cornelia

ACKNOWLEDGMENTS

Thanks to the editors of these magazines, the following poems
were first published (some of them in versions different from those
collected here, or under different titles):
The Denver Quarterly, "The Blue Dress"; *The Iowa Review*, "A Large
Heavy-Faced Woman, Pocked, Unkempt, in a Loose Dress"; *The
Nation*, "Away from You"; *The New Republic*, "Eating"; *North Amer-
ican Review*, "Five Pears or Peaches"; *Partisan Review*, "Wild-
flowers"; *Ploughshares*, "Her Love," "Make Me Hear You"; *Raccoon*,
"No Matter What Has Happened This May"; *Tendril*, "Saints";
The Yale Review, "The Eager Interpreter".

This book was completed with the help of fellowships from the
John Simon Guggenheim Memorial Foundation and the National
Endowment for the Arts, for which the author is very grateful;
thanks also to Ragdale.

© 1986 by Reginald Gibbons

For information, address the publisher:
  Persea Books
  225 Lafayette Street
  New York, N.Y. 10012

Library of Congress Cataloging-in-Publication Data
Gibbons, Reginald.
  Saints.

  (The National poetry series)
  I. Title. II. Series.
PS3557.I1392S2   1986   811'.54   86-2500
ISBN 0-89255-106-2
ISBN 0-89255-107-0 (pbk.)

Designed by Peter St. John Ginna
Set in Janson by Keystrokes, Lenox, Massachusetts
Printed by BookCrafters, Chelsea, Michigan

CONTENTS

My saints, what night does not bring me your names?
St. June, St. Jim, St. Tom, St. Sonny, St. Nell,
St. Shot-in-the-Hand, St. Mike, St. Jesse James,
St. Lingo, St. Suzanne, St. Speed, St. Al.
St. Wayne, St. Mack, Sts. Darryl and Darlene,
St. Pete, St. Joe, St. Cloud, St. Louis, St. Clair,
Sts. Mom and Dad, St. Cuffy, St. Irene,
St. Abe, St. Gloria, St. Standing Bear.
St. Marybeth, St. Catfish, St. José,
St. Wade, St. Ray, St. Bo, St. Crazy Snake,
St. Washington and St. Enola Gay,
St. Marge, St. Who, Sts. Candy, Coke and Cake.
St. Sis, St. Dick, St. Ruby, St. Adelle,
St. Sojourner, St. Nat, St. Vincent de Paul.

EATING

As if it's been waiting until he can't have it,
some moment they lived, that he didn't want
when it was his, begins to raise a craving in him—
good dinner that she used to hear him
bring thoughtfully upstairs to where
she was waiting—reading or watching TV.
They'd spend a half-hour eating it,
their familiar life was a comfort, then from
the next room where he'd be brooding
over books or just hoarding himself
he'd listen for her quiet movement,
sometimes laughter as she watched TV or read.
Did she want him to think she was happy?
But he'd sit still and ponder what
was expected of him, or hoped.
Later they'd snack, or one of them would.

Remorse now makes him remember her saying
one time when they were crying in her new
living room filled with familiar things
that were just hers, not his any more,
"I wish I'd stayed to have breakfast with you."
She meant all those mornings she had
hurried away to work, him still in bed
debating with himself whether to get up,
whether to have an egg or skip to lunch.

(Once at a dinner when they were admiring
all the work their hosts had finished together
on floors and walls, but famished, she had
told him how she liked something he had done
and he'd bitten at her, red with his own
unsuspected anger, then sick at her tears.)

It wasn't her fault he'd lain in bed.
His too-wistful asking her to stay those mornings
only showed he thought it would be easier
if she went, though there were days
he'd get up to walk to the diner
with her at that special pace they hit
together, that came to life from them
like a child, but was broken
when after breakfast he watched her go on
alone to work and he walked the other way
full of coffee and bread—

As it would break if they were tired
after those dinners with friends
when they'd eaten too much. And even if
he'd done nothing cruel, walking home
side by side late and out of step,
each could silently take back—
and he often would—what had seemed
affectionately given in the company of others.
A brief safe walk to bed—the distance
sometimes growing, the closer they got to home.

And in bed, whether they did or they didn't;
snugged against each other or not;
with the silence denying all hurts
or tears from either or both;
with him refusing to answer
or her taking a sharp
quick breath to say *yes*;
good food and too much wine
or bad and none—
                    they were hungry
lying awake, and hungry they fell asleep,
and sleeping, all night long, they were hungry.

ELSEWHERE CHILDREN

In the icy block between Madison and Monroe
walking slowly and unbalanced
by the two unequal bags of layers of
bags of apparently nothing,

she who was once somebody's darling—
and the somebody lost to her years
ago and forgotten, maybe, along with birthdays
and beatings and other things that were best

forgotten—has stopped in a doorway.
Two persons come walking by her unaware,
a young woman who is saying "There's *something*
I need, not sure what," and a young man

with goatee and thin dirty gloves
who answers, "You looking for a man to protect you!"
This woman he's been wishing for and has
just met frowns and slows down;

with her "I'm all right" they stop near
the old one's shallow niche out of the wind.
(What cold hand turned her this way? When?
Last year? Or the year she was four

or five, so long ago?) The young woman
stamps her cheap sleek boots in the salty slush
and splashes the man's wet running shoes,
she says, "I'm hungry" and he answers, hoping

maybe coffee will be enough for her, "My son says
Daddy you going to eat eggs this morning?—
I say no more, man, not no more! I heard they
really bad for you!" And he laughs down at the shoes

so useless to him, at the wonder of a world
beyond his powers. The old woman squints up at him
but the young one with him only says,
looking off, "My little girl's seven."

Separate parents, she and he, of elsewhere children.
(Where did the old woman's father leave her
one day, the start of the path here,
if just with a way of saying no or yes?)

My own dearborn, away from me today,
with secrets already of puzzling
not quite thinkable harm
(I know, because at my slight warnings

sometimes inside you a troubling echo
I can't hear alarms you, you say
"Don't tell me that or I'll worry
about it all night and I won't be able to sleep!")—

my only-five-years-old, with a soul
already taught by pain to be articulate
and beginning already to wrinkle, let no day
or disappointment ever turn you

toward a street as cold and hungry as this.
Let someone show me please how to keep
you from it if I can, if they can.
As for wishing you always free of ordinary pain,

like a father's or a mother's, I might
as well wish food into dead refrigerators
and the warmth to come out of these store-windows
into the street and do some good.

Then the young woman and man walk away.
And she who was once somebody's darling
blinks them away and gone in the between-buildings light,
they could be her children, she was once

someone's, but she can't look after them,
we can't look after our own.

MAKE ME HEAR YOU

When my Aunt Lera—tiny now,
slow moving and slow talking—
wanted to tell me about
her life, she began by saying
"Curtis and me had just one. . .
year . . . together." Curdiss
(the way she says it) was
a genial great man by all
remembrances of him, and the two
of them, just married, would go
fishing in the evening from
the banks of the Pearl,
the green stream in Mt. Olive,
Mississippi. A year of that—
quiet aloneness together
after supper, I imagine,
and the things each showed
the other, and the bed turned down—
but then Curdiss's father
came to live with them
in their tiny house and while
Curdiss was away at work
in the mill the old man would
find his way out to the yard
and have fits, twirling around,
falling, so she'd have to
pick him up and carry him

back inside, and that was
how they lived till
Curdiss died, and then his father.

Dead Curdiss is Lera's
old ghost who has flown with her
into every day, the lost chance
to live alone with him as he was
and could have been, and you're
a ghost who'll fly alongside
me into the ruins and rooms
I was the one who decided
we would never share
again—you'll hover up just
when you see the thing you want
to show me, and unable to
make me hear you, unable to hear
me say back to you, *Oh love, I would
never have seen that without you.*

for V.

NO MATTER WHAT HAS HAPPENED
THIS MAY

I love the little row of life along the low rusted garden-wire fence that divides my small city backyard from my neighbor's. The wild unruly rose, I hacked like a weed last spring; then it shot quick running lengths of vine in every direction and shuddered into a thickness of blown blossoms—the kind you can't cut and take in because they fall apart—so I think I should cut it back as if to kill it again. The violets, just beautiful weeds. Then there are yellow-green horseradish leaves, they rose as fast as dandelions in today's rain and sun; and the oregano and mint are coming back, too, you can't discourage them. Last year's dry raspberry canes are leaning, caught in the soft thorns of the new, at the corner. And beyond them, the mostly gone magnolia in the widow's yard, behind ours, the white petals on the ground in a circle like a crocheted bedspread thrown down around the black trunk.

I went out to see what the end of the day was like, away from everything, for a minute, and it was drizzling slowly. I touched the ground, just to feel it wet against my palm; and the side of the house, too. They were there. It was quiet, and I saw two robins bringing weeds and twigs to a nesting place in the new leaves at the stumpy top of a trimmed buckeye limb. How little they need—weeds and some time—to build with.

In a month I may find a new one not yet fully fledged, lost from the nest, and put it on the highest limb I can reach, but not high enough to escape harm's way, I imagine, when the harm is a shock within it, a giving up already; and it will be dead before morning. That's happened before. But these robins were just building, and one came with a full beak and paused a moment on a lower branch and cocked its head and looked upward and shifted as if it were a muscled cat, of all things, about to leap, and then it did leap and disappeared into the clump of leaves, and shook them, as the single drops of rain were gently shaking them one by one, here and there.

I was getting wet but I felt held outside because I could hear, from inside the house, a woman and a child—my wife and my daughter—laughing in the bathtub together, their laughter not meant for me but brought out to me like a gift by the damp still air so I could see that like the rain and the robins and the row of weeds they too were working and building. I'm not going to mention, now, any harm or hurt they have suffered; no winter nor summer government; no green troops nor trimmed limbs of trees; no small figures beaten or fallen. I wiped the dirt off my palms and I picked up again the glass of wine I had carried out with me. I rejoiced. There was no way not to, wet with the sound of that laughter and whispering in the last light of a day we had lived.

THE EAGER INTERPRETER

Imagining, on a long walk
between two Greek towns,
those Turkish prisoners the guidebook
says were sabred where they crowded
together on the stone dock;
and then imagining—still walking,
anxious to see some worker
in the fields or another old couple
like the last one (he riding
the donkey, she leading it in black)—
the Greeks whom the Germans shot;
and as the road after rising
leads down again, at last to
the town by the bay, imagining
all the feuds given license
by the civil war, the woman
whose husband, forgive him
his faults now, steps
dead through the doorway one night:
imagining, imagining—is there
a way out of this brooding ahead
to the hollow thud of the first
dirt thrown down on his coffin?

What is the word any tongue
can make good for the boy—
let someone else name his country—

who speaks to his sleeping wife
when he leaves at night,
his brother tagging after him,
one puny gun between them?
If his cold spirit can still
speak her name tomorrow, won't she feel
even more alone?
                    Aeneas carried
a high purpose on the point of his sword:
a city needed founding, if not
here then in another place.
This road, though, dips past
two ordinary houses and then the disco
casting a stale abandoned shade,
sharp-edged, to one side, and I descend—
through hot odd-angled streets lined
with those plane trees whose name's
so bland and awkward translated
out of sunny Greek or Spanish—
to the huge white plane-tree-shaded square.

At the cafe in the open air
I order lemonade from the waitress
who has just served the little table
crowded round by seven or eight,
a changing group—the eager interpreter
talking and listening at the same time,
three young women
dressed up, and even in this small town

the four military men from the foreign
ship offshore, out of uniform but
with an apparent eye for swag
some future day, talking of
small deals, clever braveries, travels.
They exact smiles and attentions
and never have they seen such
a pretty town as this, never.

The three women listen hard
to the roared harsh sounds of the odd tongue,
then impatiently to the interpreter
while the military men wait.
What could such noise be about?
Do these men love the ways ours do,
do they like their women
to speak to them in bed, to say
what they want, to say it?

The Turkish prisoners had been led outside
with the lie that they'd be freed.

Inside the smoky small bar so
they can watch without being watched,
young men are bitter, imagining
the weight of medals, coming
one by one to the dusty window-glass
then returning toward the far unlit interior.
The lemonade arrives at last

in the pretty hands of the waitress,
she puts it on my white table
under the plane trees and hurries away
to be near the laughing group,
foreign men who one day may bring
something new to the town, or something old.

for Gloria

TWO KINDS OF SINGING

1. After Salvador Díaz Mirón's "Example" (1901)

The public corpse was rotting on the branch
like hideous fruit that drooped against the stem;
the proof of an improbable decree,
it swayed above the road like a pendulum.

The shameless nakedness, the bulging tongue,
a shock of hair straight up like a rooster's comb—
it had the look of farce; and a ragged gang
of boys, all jokes, stood grinning by my horse.

And the mournful sack of guts, with head bowed down,
swollen outrage on the green hanging tree,
vented a putrid stench in the strong gusts
as like a censer in solemn arcs it swung.
And the sun was rising through a flawless blue:
Tibullus put such landscape into song.

2. *After Osip Mandelstam (#54, 1913)*

Bread that's poisoned, and not a sip of air,
how hard it is to get a wound to heal.
Joseph himself, sold to Egypt to slave,
could not have been more heavily grieved.

But under starry skies the Bedouins come,
they still their horses, and with eyes closed
invent a story—a rambling epic poem
of the vague day they've lived through, almost bored.

Among them, little's needed to inspire—
who lost a quiver in the sand,
how a trade of geldings went—events
are a mist that starts to thin and disappear.

And if the song is sung out to the end,
wholeheartedly, with all the breath in the lungs,
everything vanishes—and what remains
is the vast space, the stars, the one who sings.

FRIDAY SNOW

Something needs to be done—like dragging a big black plastic sack through the upstairs rooms, emptying into it each waste basket, the trash of three lives for a week or so. I am careful and slow about it, so that this little chore will banish the big ones. But I leave the bag lying on the floor and I go into my daughter's bedroom, into the north morning light from her windows, and while this minute she is at school counting or spelling a first useful word I sit down on her unmade bed and I look out the windows at nothing for a while, the unmoving buildings—houses and a church—in the cold street.

Across it a dark young man is coming slowly down the white sidewalk with a snowshovel over his shoulder. He's wearing a light coat, there's a plastic shower-cap under his dirty navy blue knit hat, and at a house where the walk hasn't been cleared he climbs the steps and rings the doorbell and stands waiting, squinting sideways at the wind. Then he half wakes and he says a few words I can't hear to the storm door that doesn't open, and he nods his head with the kindly farewell that is a habit he wears as disguise, and he goes back down the steps and on to the next house. All of this in pantomime, the way I see it through windows closed against winter and the faint sounds of winter.

My daughter's cross-eyed piggy bank is also star-ing out blankly, and in its belly are four dollar bills that came one at a time from her grandmother and which tomorrow she will pull out of the corked mouth-hole. (It's not like the piggy banks you have to fill before you empty them because to empty them you have to smash them.) Tomorrow she will buy a perfect piece of small furniture for her warm well-lit dollhouse where no one is tired or weak and the wind can't get in.

Sitting on her bed, looking out, I didn't see a bundled-up lame child out of school and even turned out of the house for a while, or a blind woman with burns or a sick bald veteran—people who might have walked past stoop-shouldered with what's happened and will keep happening to them. So much limping is not from physical pain—the pain is gone now, but the leg's still crooked. The piggy bank and I see only the able young man whose straight back nobody needs.

When he finally gets past where I can see him, it feels as if a kind of music has stopped, and it's more completely quiet than it was, an emptiness more than a stillness, and I get up from the rumpled bed and I smooth the covers, slowly and carefully, and I look around the room for something to pick up or straighten, and I take a wadded dollar bill from my pocket and put it into the pig and I walk out.

FIVE PEARS OR PEACHES

Buckled into the cramped back seat, she sings to herself as I drive toward her school. Straining upward to see out her window, she watches the things that go by, the ones she sees—I know only that some of them are the houses we sometimes say we wish were ours. But today as we pass them we only think it; or I do, while she's singing—the big yellow one with a roofed portico for cars never there, the pink stucco one with red shutters that's her favorite. Most of what she sings rhymes as it unwinds in the direction she goes with it. Half the way to school she sings, and then she stops, the song becomes a secret she'd rather keep to herself, her underground sweetwater stream through the tiny continent of her, on which her high oboe voice floats through forests softly, the calling of a hidden pensive bird—this is the way I strain my grasp to imagine what it's like for her to be thinking of things, to herself, to be feeling her happiness or fear.

After I leave her inside the school, which was converted from an old house in whose kitchen you can almost still smell the fruit being cooked down for canning, she waves good-bye from a window, and I can make her cover her mouth with one hand and laugh and roll her eyes at a small classmate if I cavort a little down the walk.

In some of her paintings, the sun's red and has teeth, but the houses are cheerful, and fat flying birds with almost human faces and long noses for beaks sail downward toward the earth, where her giant bright flowers overshadow like trees the people she draws.

At the end of the day, her naked delight in the bath is delight in a lake of still pleasures, a straight unhurried sailing in a good breeze, and a luxurious trust that there will always be this calm warm weather, and someone's hand to steer and steady the skiff of her. Ashore, orchards are blooming.

Before I get into bed with her mother at night, I look in on her and watch her sleeping hands come near her face to sweep away what's bothering her dreaming eyes. I ease my hand under her back and lift her from the edge of the bed to the center. I can almost catch the whole span of her shoulders in one hand—five pears or peaches, it might be, dreaming in a delicate basket—till they tip with their own live weight and slip from my grasp.

HER LOVE

A man whose son has died has
to forgive the boys who
still live, when they come
up the street slowly in
a ragged group, talking, three
with mitts, one with the ball.
Should forgive, and does.
Because whatever first trust there was
in anything is gone now, anyway,

and what he could never think
of losing has been lost.
But the woman he loves
says we are not cups poured empty
and there's no measure in being mad.
So when she offers him what
she can, her love, he takes it
greedily, thankfully, glad.

THAT PHONE CALL

You were saying the radio that cold morning
had come on early, but with bird-song,
the dawn chorus, people call it

(while here the silent chill was falling
over my bed from the warped window as I still slept—
still dim here, lighter where you were).

Summer songs in the stiff morning!
You'd waked Katie and said, Listen.
And you'd cried at being alive and healing

while new tumors had come up, you'd heard,
beneath your good friend's papery scars.
The day got worse (that waiting, then, was bad,

things we couldn't resolve were holding
the peace we wanted away from us like a handful
of medicine we felt we had to have)

but the sun shone for a while, you said,
cars came and went on the icy road.
I listened, I could see your shoulders,

the kitchen fluorescence like black-and-white
over you and the letters and the cigarettes
and cold coffee cup by the telephone.

I'm down, you said, I'm tired, I'm blue
again, help me get to sleep.
I could see your black hair, your mouth,

your legs inside your warm robe.
I couldn't help seeing them!
It was dark here when we spoke, darker there.

We couldn't harmonize on "she'll
be comin' round the mountain when
she comes" for Kate's delight, or sit

still talking to each other after
her bedtime, or, coming closer, touch.
What you would be able to do for your friend

was going to be hard and it wouldn't save her.
It's no use, you said, I'll hang up.
Don't, I said, wait a little longer,

and the bridge of an old love-song
I'd been trying for days to remember
came to me then, tightening my throat

around the tune as if I'd never
lost it or worried I'd forget, and I said
Sing this song to me, it's not

too soon for you to start singing
us all awake, let song carry
the blue away till we can be together,

wait, I'm listening, sing—
you sing it and I'll sing too.

THE VANISHING POINT

A young man with bad teeth and a walleyed gaze, holding some poster boards on his lap, where they sagged at each side, and drawing on the top one with an old chewed ballpoint pen.

It was a severely rectilinear highway scene: a powerful exaggerated vanishing point puckering the empty horizon, lanes of cars coming on—as yet only outlined—and lanes of big trucks going away, already finished. One after another, all alike, semi-trailers with company names on them, and all the perspective acutely correct. It all looked to have been drawn with a ruler, strictly and slowly; but he was doing it freehand, each stroke of the pen absolutely precise. Or rather, as imprecise as the human hand, but with the true authority of a technical mastery that could convey and even create precision in your eyes as you looked. Even the lettering he was putting on the side of the last, closest, largest trailer was as if painted by machine, and he never paused to consider proportions or angles, but simply kept drawing and darkening the shapes with the blue pen, as if he were tracing—and with quick uncanny dash—a faint design already there on the white floppy board.

This was at Chicago and State, in the subway station.

A woman happened to come and stand near him, and watched as he worked with his intent rhythm, his head bobbing and sometimes with his face low to study his work closely with one eye at a time. She watched, and he noticed her and smiled a wreck-toothed wide blind man's smile at her, and said, more than asked, "Nice work, idn't it!" She put her right thumb up and smiled back at him, and said nothing, and he lifted the top board and showed her the finished one underneath, for an instant—another roadscape, in colors, filled in and alive, the whole huge white board crammed with convincing and convinced detail.

"Nice work, idn't it!" he said again, and showed her the one underneath that one. Again, thumb up, and she too smiled happily, a wholly natural acknowledgment of him, an unsurprised understanding of his talent. She didn't act as if it seemed strange to her that he was sitting on a worn drab bench on the subway platform, next to the tracks, working in the dim light while commuters and others stood around waiting impatiently for the next train. It didn't seem to strike her that he was crazy and half-blind. That his work was driven, obsessively scrupulous, uninhabited, repetitive, brilliant, rhythmical, depthless, spiritless, useless.

"Nice work, idn't it!" he said to her each time, and he showed her—and me, because I too was standing there—six or eight more drawings: the Sears Tower, the skyline along Michigan Ave., traffic in the streets, not a single person. The long lines were perfectly straight but when you looked at them more carefully they zigged with freehand force across the board in spurts. And her thumb went up to each in turn, and she smiled and each time she did, he said, "Nice work, idn't it!"

"I do nice work!" he said. "I did *all* these, and not a *single mistake!* Nice work!" he was saying as the train came in like sandpaper, hissing and blasting. She walked away toward it, without saying good-bye, and he looked at me, then. "Nice work, idn't it!" he said, as cheerfully as a man could ever say it.

"It's *beautiful!*" I said. The doors to the train opened a few feet away and everyone was stepping inside. "It's nice *work!*" he said, smiling, and I moved to the train and stepped in, with the great force in him holding me to him still, and with part of myself I wished that it would win, but I did get in, the last passenger, and the doors shut at the same moment the train jerked and began to roll out of the station and away.

DUTCH THURSDAY MORNINGS

It makes a picture: the skies
have a lather in them over
the leaden dimness, the small figures

in the foreground are frenzied
at going, frightened to go,
on the platform beside
the still train they cry to each other
for help no one who would give, can,
and which those who can, will not.

(Seeing them even in the mind
you need a kind of anesthetic.
But there's none strong enough
that you can also be brought back from.)

To keep from thinking about
what they know about—
but involuntarily
chasing their screaming
thoughts of it—
they stayed up all night carefully
packing the knapsacks and bags
they don't know they won't be given
the great and human privilege of keeping.

(The pane of glass of passed time

between you and them—
as if you couldn't hear them calling
from beyond it, you can only see
their mouths moving, their fists beating the empty air—
makes you begin to feel a cold empty hollow place
growing under your collarbone,
an icy trickle that leaks from your shoulders
into the useless muscles of your limp arms,
into your fingers that couldn't grip anything,
that can't make a fist and rise
to smash the pane of glass.)

On the third level of bunks
the only male in the barracks, a boy,
was sleeping. A woman
lay on the second, awake and silent,
and standing beside the first
an exempted friend was shoving
some dry bread into a corner of their
ridiculously handsome suitcase.

In the very smallest driest crust of bread
a tiny hope could still prosper,
flitting like a candleflame
that could make a man flinch blind
or send a woman into a mesmerized
daze of insane helplessness.

(Doctor? You said I wouldn't feel anything.)

Look, what a good heavy overcoat!
And where they are going, not even
a thin white sheet for wrapping round the body.

Let them go, then.
You can't stop it.
The sky is changing, it would take
a great painter to capture it.
And those lucky enough to have
to wait another week walk
back to their barracks with a metal
taste on their tongues,
a bitter foul scent around them,
and they feel the sunlight—
they squint up at it as if somehow
it could betray them, and had—
they feel the sunlight finally
come on like a surgical lamp
over the autopsy table they're not allowed
even to die on.

WILDFLOWERS

Coleridge carefully wrote down a whole page
of them, all beginning with the letter b.
Guidebooks preserve our knowledge
of their hues and shapes, their breeding.
Many poems have made delicate word-chimes—
like wind-chimes not for wind but for the breath of man—
out of their lovely names.
At the edge of the prairie in a cabin
when thunder comes closer to thump the roof hard
a few of them—in a corner, brittle in a dry jar
where a woman's thoughtful hand left them to fade—
seem to blow with the announcing winds outside
as the rain begins to fall on all their supple kin
of all colors, under a sky of one color, or none.

APRIL TO MAY

Innumerable fresh starts of which
nothing or little needs to be made
have built a heap of possibilities
for me, for nearly anyone
since a day two weeks ago
that marked the death of a friend.
It's too soon to be surprised
to see the paper scrap still
pinned above desk and letters and photos—
name and telephone number
of this woman who has died.

It would be a comfort,
almost, to have followed—instead
of her slow decline, that made her
lurch and trip along the path
the rest of us miraculously walked—
the surprising inevitable fall
of a good sad story in which
the troublesome colt is finally
shot by a passing soldier, or the heroine's
left to die—she insists
that the others go on—
by the river in flood.

But what happened to my friend
was not a good story, nothing

in the sad ending's right.
Or rather, she and her suffering
ended and the story didn't
stop for her. Everywhere
alphabets are all still
in use, small children easily
speak what foreigners won't master
with the years of practice to come,
there are acts and letters of new
apostles, the struggles against them
continue. It's raining today.
Lice and azaleas and racehorses
are flourishing. The May light's
lengthening into the nights
she no longer sleeps in.

Her attempts and hopes, the air
in her rooms that lifted
her scent to me when she passed,
and her voice—nothing of her
is moving with the fast current,
everything of her drifts to a stillness,
left in an eddy with all
that's finished, a dry leaf
on the water, deepening,
while every real living
one of us has rushed a little
farther these few minutes,

afloat with our grief and opportunity,
still calling back—

hours of her, days,
                    April to May.

AWAY FROM YOU

Sounds of crickets and chickadees
A wasp crawling on the inside of the porch screen
Plaintive small whistle of a white-crowned sparrow
Morning cicadas in the trees by the hot garden
I think of holding gently a tight fistful of your
     black hair and kissing you
A house chair left outside in the sun by the tomatoes
You stood me before the doors I'd kept closed
A jay honking and lecturing, won't stop, in the
     cedars—like me
A huge black ant wobbling by as it carries another
You have been the way that was opened for me
Motionless planks slanted against the cabin-side
     and an empty tin bucket under them
Against you I've limped till I could walk again
     and then beside you walked
Till hurt and limping; and stayed, even when
     you did the hurting
Whatever wildflower blossom you are, I'm still
     not sure of your name
Weathered wood, new blooms, quiet peace, leaning
     tree, the open cabin door

Everything, when I am in my thoughts of you,
    begins to signify
I want to be, I want to have been
    what you have been for me
For you

C.

AMERICAN TRAINS

The Santa Fe, still the one
        that most often sings me its name;
and the rattling Erie & Lackawanna
        that used to ride my first love—
        in whose bed I cried with the thought
        no days would ever be long enough for us—
        to Pennsylvania and school, far
        before I had tried her attention,
        truly, or her forgiveness;
and the always late AMTRAK Montrealer
        that stopped in Massachusetts cornfields
        one night to wait for all the stars
        and American clocks to catch up to it
        as Daylight Savings came on;
and the smoky Conrail commuter
        that rocked and screeched through chemical air
        to New York, a rolling lurching urinal
        carrying bankers and middlemen
        and secretaries smoothing
        their weekday best and putting new lipstick on
        as we coasted out of the tunnel
        into Penn Station and waited—standing
        jammed together with salesmen whose sportcoats
        would never hang right from their tired shoulders,
        and teachers needing new heels, and lawyers—
        waited for the doors to open onto the hot black
            platform;

and the relic locomotive and open cars
        careening a few miles for tourists in New Jersey,
        the steam engine shocking eyes
        with smoke and coal motes, flushing pheasants
        gaudy with mating out of the trackside brush
        on the back side of shopping centers;
and there's the one you and I got on,
        that started downhill with the weight
        of what we felt and is still in a plummet,
        always and always faster till it has us shaking,
        out of breath, scared. . . "A *freight* train,"
        I said when you asked me, "What *is* this?"

A LARGE HEAVY-FACED WOMAN,
POCKED, UNKEMPT, IN A LOOSE DRESS

. . . and her mute shadow touching me
made me look up, the glass panes
and squatting aircraft like a movie screen
behind her, and she smiled, held out
a small orange card that I took
with my hand from her hand—

the deaf-and-dumb alphabet on one side,
hand-signs, and on the other her plea,
her exhortation, her prayer, her pitch:
SMILE. With the fingers that took my coins
she drew a blessing in the air and
like a tired usher walked away
down the empty seats and dirty ashtrays

to a young woman with a baby, the orange
card hovered till the child stirred,
reaching up, reaching, the mother lifted
her head from her worries to frown,
say no. Maybe someone was late.
Or hadn't caught the right plane or had
caught it, leaving; or left with bad words.

The big woman shaped another smile with her lips,
touched the baby's curling wafting hand,
traced her blessing again, wasted no words.

[45]

Her limp fingers invisible with the silence
of their stillness, down the narrowing corridor
she went toward the next gate, where some
gathered oblivious drunk traveling men

wearing cowboy hats and boots after their convention
were singing the loud song she couldn't hear
as she approached them like the stage messenger
whose surprising words will signal the end but
who says nothing this time, and the singing stops,
the actors stand in place waiting and the audience,
restless and embarrassed, begin to bark into their hands

willing now to welcome any word, even the bad news
The Queen is dead or The old shepherd
whom you summoned knows or I alone escaped to tell thee.
But she doesn't speak, only her hands can—like yours,
you accoutered conventioneers and young grievers,
you tired mothers, you healers and whores on trips,
wife-beaters and tormentors of children,

you shoe-salesmen, cooks, polite cold freeway toll-takers
with warm palms, you men making fists
in your compulsive pockets around coins or keys,

you women groping in purses for cigarettes,
for candy and gum and lipstick confused,
here is your herald! Some message is come.
Even the worst she can say will be touching.

And your being still could be a kind of listening.

HOLLISTER ROAD

Sometimes I wish I had not changed so many times the way I see things, and I could still hold to an earlier way, perhaps one less stunned, slower to guard itself against what it may see.

To recover it even for a moment would require working back in memory and trying to forget my first sight of mountains, from a Greyhound in New Mexico, summer I was seventeen. And to reach that point, first I'd have to rid myself of the Pacific Ocean, of scabby-ankled men in broken shoes on hot city streets, of the slave-labor kilns I saw in one far country, and in another, the summer view from the saint's church at dusk when the distant village lights started coming on in the valley below, and of all the other images I have preserved, wanting to and no, with a camera in my mind, that are always coming back at unexpected moments when I can't see the connection between where I am, what I'm doing, and all of a sudden what I see.

I would also have to forget the little commercial enterprises and small houses modeled on inappropriate, but perhaps forgivable, grandiosities, that came to crowd our road eventually like warts along the vein of a smooth, plain hand. Everyone was building a house, then. And I would have to restore a field of ordinary weeds, where freeway builders dug a huge straight-sided quarry hole for sand and gravel, a pit so huge it suggested a cataclysm. When they were finished digging, it filled with clear greenish water in which nothing ever lived but algae, and finally it had to be called a "lake," and posted against trespassers, when the new houses had come close to it and someone's child, swimming there, had drowned.

I have to go back before all that, to the moment when our house was the last on the road, in a place with few trees, and I can remember some birds—doves, quail, bobwhite, meadowlarks, redbirds. There were killdeer tracks, delicate, as if carefully drawn, in the fine white silt after rain, when the dampness would hold the impression till the hot sun dried everything out again and the dust drifted softly over itself.

I saw a photograph taken a century ago, a man in a suit lying awkwardly at the far side of the only unusual spot in a flat landscape where it's miles and miles from one tree or house to the next: a shallow small concavity, a sink hole, perhaps twenty feet broad and not more than four feet deep at the center. The grand natural curiosity of that locale? The man is posing beside it, with more of the vacant expanse beyond him and in front of him than the rectangular photo could show, and so perhaps he has a greater sense of how truly odd and noteworthy the sink hole is. He has brought his photographer all the way out from town to take the picture. It's his trophy. And it's something that would make the experienced traveler only laugh. It's not a something, but a kind of nothing. And yet once, at least, a man got down on his side, propped himself on his elbow, and held still for the camera, there. . . .

I want to show you the fresh small tracks of the killdeer. On an afternoon of a breeze, after a black and green thunderstorm, when the torrents might have filled the ditch next to our house and spilled into the yard so you couldn't tell any more where the bank dropped off ten feet—on that kind of an afternoon, when the air seemed newly created and never yet used for anything, my mother might hand each of us a plastic bowl and say go across to the field and pick some dewberries and I'll make a cobbler for dinner. And don't track mud into the house when you come back! We crossed the ditch on the two-lane wooden bridge that was still there, then, before it was torn away and replaced with a wider, concrete one, with railings, and the name of some mayor.

I would need to forget that new bridge to get back to what I'm trying to see, and I'd need to remember that after big rains it was wonderful to lie belly-down on the wooden bridge, hang your head over the edge and watch the murky flood go dizzying by. I'd have to forget that many years later I learned that the deep ditch around Mycenae was called Chaos.

On the other side of the ditch we entered the empty field by slipping through the rusty slack barbed-wire fence, and always cast a glance over at the ten or twelve good big trees in the next field beyond the berry field, a kind of grove, so strange in the wide emptiness. It was a mysterious place we sometimes visited—such a stadium of shade, so unnatural, seemed to have an elusive meaning. I wish I could show you the etched tracks of the killdeer, a bird that runs along the ground. Going to and from the grove, too, we'd find them beside the shallow slicks of rain on the flat bare sun-bleached earth, in the wide spaces between clumps of wire-grass and yaupon bushes. And in the berry field, around the mounds of tangled stickerbushes where the dewberries grew wild, heavy and freshened by rain. We rarely came close to a killdeer, but sometimes one would cry off taking flight ahead of us as we tramped.

To us those tracks were a hushing, stopping proof of wild life as much as the sight of a lion would have been, and the sharp-scented air made us alert for every such trace as we picked berries and got tiny blood scratches on our wrists and hands. It was possible to spot a horned toad, too, or some kind of small snake, *stay out of its way.* The breeze would fail after a while, and as soon as the air was still and warm again the bugs would return up into it. We could pick quarts of berries in a short time and they cooked down so much we needed to get a lot, and then we'd run back and deliver them, and wait for dinner and dessert.

I'd like to have stayed behind, though, just once, till the others were through the fence, back over the bridge, and gone, and then to have lain down beside the small rain-slick with my white plastic bowl of black berries, next to the killdeer's pronged footprints, and told my photographer to open the shutter on me there.

MONEY

The children are eating lunch at home on a summer weekday when a man comes to the door and asks their mother if she has anything that needs fixing or carrying or any yardwork he can do. They chew their food a little dreamily as, with her back straight and her voice carefully polite, she says No, thank you, I'm sorry, and the man goes away. Who was that, Mama? they say. Oh, no one, she says.

They are sitting down to dinner but they have to wait because the doorbell rings and a thin young boy begins to tell their father about a Sales Program he's completing for a scholarship to be Supervisor, and he holds up a filthy tattered little booklet and lifts also his desperate guile and heavily guarded hope, and the children's father says, No thank you, sorry but I can't help you out this time, and the boy goes away. The children start to eat and don't ask anything, because the boy was just a boy, but their father acts irritated and hasty when he sits back down.

Once a glassy-eyed heavy girl who almost seems asleep as she stands outside their door offers for sale some little handtowels stitched by the blind people at the Lighthouse for the Blind and the children are in the folds of their mother's full skirt listening to the girl's small voice and their mother says, Well, I bought some the last time.

She buys the children school supplies and food,

she pays the two boys for mowing the yard together and weeding her flower bed. She gets a new sewing machine for her birthday from the children's father, and she buys fabric and thread and patterns and makes dresses for the girls, to save money. She tells the children each to put a dime or quarter into the collection plate at Church, and once a month she puts in a little sealed white envelope, and the ushers move slowly along the ends of the pews weaving the baskets through the congregation, and the organist plays a long piece of music.

Whisk brooms, magazine subscriptions, anything you need hauled away, little league raffle tickets, cookies, chocolate candy, can I do any yard work again and again, hairbrushes, Christmas cards, do you need help with your ironing one time, and more, came calling at the front door while the children were sometimes eating, sometimes playing. Their faces would soften with a kind of comfort in the authority of mother or father, with a kind of wonder at the needy callers.

Their father left for work every day early, and came home for dinner, and almost always went again on Saturday; in his car. Their mother opened a savings account for each child and into each put the first five dollars. The children felt proud to see their names in the passbooks, and wanted to know when they could take the money out. But they were told they had to save their money not spend it. They felt a kind of pleasure in these mysteries, to know that there were things you would understand later when you grew up and had your own house and while your children were eating their dinner and making too much noise the way you did, you knew it was true, the doorbell would ring, the familiar surprise of it, who would it be, and someone would be holding a little worn book or a bundle of dishtowels or once an old man, but perhaps he only looked old, with his beard, came with bunches of carnations, white, red, and pink, and he too was turned away.

SAINTS

*All violent people secretly desire
to be curbed by something that they
respect, so that they may become
known to themselves.*
Allen Tate

*O that thou shouldst give dust a tongue
To cry to thee
And then not hear it crying!*
George Herbert

1. THE BLUE DRESS

You tore it off my back.

But I'm not good
at telling a story—you'd shut
me up by saying that—
so I guess I can't tell this one,
that had to do with the way
I once used to feel
when someone like you
who had done a rough kind
of work—work that can kill you
if you're not careful—talked
to me like my listening
was important to him.
                    And listened
to me, too, made me feel
I could be the gentleness
he needed after bad
times—someone who'd grown
up hard and alone, like you,
or gotten through the war
alive. . . But I don't feel
the same about you any
more, or nearly anyone,
any man, I've known.
I thought when I met you
and it was exciting to me

to be with you, it was
more life I was getting—
and it was less.

But you said I was special,
I was the best of all
the girls—the women—you'd had,
the sexiest, I turned you on
the most. That's what I'd
remember when I'd want
to leave you, when you'd been
after me again, like always
drunk, hunting me or saying
you'd kill me. I'd try remembering
that nobody else ever told me
I was special or beautiful,
and I thought it was loving
me that made you say it—
I know I'm not pretty
the way some women are,
the way some were that you
would look at twice and make
me forget what you'd done
and want you for myself again.

But it was just being
scared that kept me from leaving,
you saw to that many times.

And I did used to love you,
I did love your kisses,
love that touch you had for me,
holding my face in your hands,
squeezing my shoulders for me,
the way you'd rub my tired legs
and how you'd put your hands
on my breasts, that was so careful,
I thought, not to hurt.
And my gripping you as hard
to me as I could, and you'd
say I was the best of all
of them, the best and the best
till the waves of it hit—
I'd float for a long
second or two and then it
slams through, so sweet.

But you'd hit me. Just sitting
together in the apartment and you'd
jump up and hit me yelling
"Don't do that!" and I don't
even know what it is.
You used your belt on me,
you threw me down the stairs
more than once and locked
me out alone for hours
and I never knew anyone
in the building who I could

go to, I'd just stay down
near the front door inside,
people would come in and go out
and hold the door for me
but I'd say no, I was
waiting for someone. . .

Till you came down to look.
When you made up to me
I was so happy to have
you back—back to yourself—
and we'd go out dancing,
you'd know everybody there
and those friends of yours would always
pretend that nothing's wrong.
I felt grateful to them
for treating me so friendly,
so polite, so respectful. Nice.
And they could laugh with me
in a way you couldn't, or wouldn't.

The preacher says to talk.
So I do and he listens
and doesn't say very much.
He still thinks that all
the bad came from you, that
everything bad that was done,
you did—which I'm not going
to tell him any different.

All he knows about that
night is you chased me
downstairs and into the street
at 3 a.m. with me
in my nightgown in the cold and no shoes
and you with the big kitchen
knife in your hand, yelling
you were going to cut me.

You never even knew how
afraid I was to go
to sleep and afraid to wait up
for you, too, but what would
you have cared, in those moods—
I went crazy wondering
what you'd do when you came in,
turning like a mean dog
and trying to get me when you
could barely stand up and had
to hold onto the furniture
to walk across the room.

I don't know how you
were able all of a sudden
to move so fast that night,
the state you were in, and the knife
in your hand. Then when you stopped
in the middle of the dead
street and said it was over

and turned around and started
back, I don't know why
I followed you home, either.

I watched you real carefully
when you got into bed
with your clothes on and you put
the knife under your pillow
and said to me that if I
wanted to kill you while you
were sleeping, there it was.

I waited one more hour
watching the clock go slow,
afraid you'd wake up
sick out of your alcohol sleep
and with one of your nightmares.
Then I had to reach under
your pillow to find the knife
and I cut my finger on it—
I almost cried out
but I realized that what I was
was so mad at you that
all of a sudden I wanted
to beat you hard as I could
with my fists and scream and it
still makes me crazy and I
wish I had done it—
instead. But I didn't

make a sound, just held
my cut finger that I couldn't
look at and looked at you
for a long time, trying
to guess where in you was your heart.

I had a thought and I
went back to the kitchen to put
a bandage on my cut and hold
it till it stopped bleeding
and only throbbed and I called
the police. Come over here
right now, I told them, I'm
going to kill him, and I gave
the address, the apartment,
the floor, the bedroom... I wanted
a bunch of them in case
they had to save me from
what you might do while you
were dying.
                    Or maybe what
I wanted was what they did.

I took the knife and went
first to unlock the door
for when they'd come, wondering
how long it would be. I stood
in the doorway to our room
counting to two hundred

in my mind and then counted
again, and heard them stamping
and running up the stairs
so loud I thought they'd wake you
and I ran to stab your chest
holding the knife in both hands.

It slipped sideways and tore
your shirt down your ribs
and only cut you some.
You jumped and opened your eyes
but it didn't seem like you
could see me and I stabbed you
again and it slipped again,
I couldn't make it go
into you, but too late to stop.

When the cops pulled you off
of me—I don't know where
the knife went—know what?
I had to run onto the back
landing outside and pull
the door shut, that always
locks, lock myself out
because you were yelling
Help me, Esther, help me
please God Esther, help,
they're killing me, Esther!
I would have gone back

and killed those cops to get
them off of you.

Then the noise was gone away.
I was trying to figure out
how to get back in, freezing
and crying in my nightgown,
they must have taken you away
and what would happen to you
and how could I get you out
somehow when I heard two shots
from the street around front.
I don't know what they've said
you did—when they came up
calling for me and let me
into our place and told me
what had happened to you
I couldn't seem to hear them.

What I thought of while they
were talking and talking and waiting
for me to say something
that I wasn't going to say
was how I'd last seen one
of them at your back holding
you by the collar the way
you grabbed mine the night
you tore my new blue dress
that you couldn't tell from silk

right off my back, left me
naked in a corner with my hands
up and you yelling at me
I spent too much of your money,
said I wouldn't leave you alone,
made me get in the closet
and locked me in there, shouted
through the door if I ever
tried to leave you you would
cut me so bad, no one
would want me, while I cried
into a torn rag of my dress,
all ruined and lost and wasted.

That was for you, that dress,
to make you happy, make
you want to be with me.
All I had was a physical
need in my body, for you,
and wanting you to say
you loved me and be nice
the way you used to be.
I kept thinking that if
I was nicer to you
you'd get better, you'd be
all right again, and I'd
be special to you, like before.

Now nothing can change ever
between us, we'll always
be stuck where we were that night.
Only I'm the only one
to feel it, you can't.

The preacher will tell me I
should forgive you now,
should let it go, should come
to church once in a while,
I look at him and see
another man looking at me.
You used to tell all your
stories to your friends, the hard
knocks you'd had—you said
harder than mine. Is this
story good enough, you think,
for me to tell it? But you
aren't listening, you can't
answer me, you never did,
you're not here but you won't
go away, and you can't
give me back what you took
if you're dead. If you could
give me back that one dress
then you could give me everything,
even the way one time you put
your hand in my hair after
you had hit me and said

please don't cry, sugar, don't,
honey, stop crying, please,
I promise to you that
I'll never do it ever again.

2. A PERSONAL NEED

Someone is worrying me and troubling my mind,
  bring me the mail

DO NOT OPEN THIS "CONFIDENTIAL MAIL"
UNLESS YOU LIVE AT THIS ADDRESS

DEAR FRIEND IN CHRIST I'VE READ IT IN THE BIBLE
I RE-READ IT AND I PRAYED ABOUT IT AND I'VE HEARD
THE VOICE OF THE LORD SPEAKING TO MY HEART CONCERNING
YOU AND A NEED THAT YOU HAVE IN YOUR LIFE
I SAID "LORD OVER THE YEARS YOU HAVE SENT
DIFFERENT PEOPLE TO ME I KNOW YOU DID
AND LORD I'M PRAYING THAT YOU WILL SEND "THIS FAMILY"
THE SAME TYPE OF BLESSING THAT YOU DID
FOR OUR DEAR BROTHER RAYMOND WHEN HE NEEDED
THAT TWO THOUSAND DOLLAR MIRACLE LORD REMEMBER
HOW HE PROVED TO YOU ACCORDING TO MALACHI THREE TEN

> *Bring ye all the tithes into the storehouse*
> *that there may be meat in mine house*
> *and prove me now herewith saith the Lord*
>   *of hosts*
> *if I will not open you the windows of heaven*
> *and pour you out a blessing*
> *that there shall not be room enough to receive it*

WITH THAT TWENTY DOLLARS THAT HE NEEDED AND
  THEN LORD
YOU TURNED AROUND AND BLESSED HIM WITH TWO THOUSAND
I SAID "LORD I'M ASKING YOU TO DO
THE SAME THING THE SAME TYPE OF MIRACLE
FOR MY DEAR FRIENDS IN CHRIST AT THIS ADDRESS

> Dear Prayer Family
> Yes I do have personal problems
> and I want to learn how to meet these PROBLEMS
> through PRAYER and ask that God will
> bless me with more "Good Fortune" in life
> through your new SPIRITUAL PACKAGE
> Here is the "Blessed Faith Handkerchief" back
> I've slept on it for "1" night and
> I've printed my name in the middle of it, by faith.

> > *And God wrought special miracles by the hands*
> > *of Paul so that from his body were brought*
> > *unto the sick handkerchiefs or aprons*
> > *and the disease departed from them*
> > *and the evil spirits went out of them*

NOW WHEN I GET THIS HANDKERCHIEF BACK FROM YOU
(WITH YOUR NAME ON IT) I AM GOING TO TAKE
THIS VERY SPECIAL "FAITH HANDKERCHIEF" AND PRAY
FOR A SPECIAL MIRACLE FOR YOU. I AM ASKING YOU
TO HELP US WITH OUR IMPORTANT MINISTRY
AND TELL US WHICH OF THESE PROBLEMS ARE AFFECTING YOU

1. I have a financial need in my life
   I need God to bless me with some money
      for a certain need

2. I have a personal need in my life
   Someone has hurt me
   I have a physical need in my body

3. Someone is worrying me and troubling my mind

I AM ASKING YOU RIGHT NOW TO GET OUT FIVE DOLLARS
AND GIVE IT TO THE WORK OF JESUS CHRIST

Dear Reverend I requested prayer that my husband
stop drinking It happened I'm so happy Thank Jesus

Dear Reverend My daughter has changed and is living
a new life in Jesus and service to the Lord

Dear Reverend In my prayer request I asked
for my job back Thank God I got a new one better

Dear Reverend My two boys got saved and one
filled with the Holy Ghost Praise Jesus

YOU WILL NOT NEED IT AFTER TONIGHT
RETURN IT TO ME IN THE MORNING I REPEAT
DO NOT KEEP THIS "FAITH HANDKERCHIEF"
AND PLEASE DO NOT BREAK THIS FLOWING OF GOD'S

SPIRIT FROM MY HOME TO YOUR HOME
RUSH THIS "FAITH HANDKERCHIEF" BACK
FOR I MUST WRITE YOU SOMETHING IN THE SPIRIT
THAT'S COMING TO YOUR DOOR

                              I'M ASKING YOU

3. WHERE THE GREEN GULF

Someone is worrying me and troubling my mind.
Shall I tell you about her?

They had the Christmas spirit,
went out partying till late.

> *Where the green Gulf*
> *slops out of its shallow dish*
> *praise sands for tilting up*
> *to contain it, Praise!*
> *Where somehow roadbuilders*
> *let go the cutting of liveoaks*
> *curse the trees*
> *that crowded in at the curve*
> *and caught the car*
> *when it swung wide, Move*
> *your lips in a curse!*

I thank God she died fast
and didn't suffer or become
a vegetable, like they say.
But it was bad luck, real bad

> *where the green Gulf*
> *sloshes over sand and jetties*

Someone is troubling my mind

that once used to go with me
to fish from the far end
of number six where the channel
is not too far out
and the good fish will bite.
Someone that used to come, too,
that liked fishing, out there
at the end where there wasn't
usually many others, someone
I took there when she was little—
she'd drop a string in the water
raw bacon tied to the end
and would bring up a crab
real slow so it wouldn't
let go and she'd get
sunburned and wear my hat
and now it's her that's worrying me
and I pray she's found her rest.

(I feel like I need
someone to turn to
to get over this sorrow
Lord, to be full
reconciled with your will
that took her away
when I hadn't ever thought
that she wouldn't live
beyond my days

that seem too long now
being longer than hers.)

> *Where the shallow Gulf tips*
> *in its bowl with each wave*
> *the water studies its way in*
> *through pilings, under the pier*
> *the ripples cross and crisscross*
> *like a thick reflected light*
> *that smells cold against*
> *the summer heat, smells of*
> *fish and creosote and floats*
> *the frail shells toward shore*
> *then pours back into its bowl—*
> *where the Gulf does this,*
> *and some praise its mild green,*
> *a man rests in the hard sun*
> *and wipes his face with a handkerchief*
> *that falls from his hand and's gone.*
> *And the water troubles him, sure,*
> *but the most troubled is his will.*
> *What he wishes he'd had is luck,*
> *and not even for himself.*
> *But luck just makes his misery*
> *seem to come from some past mistake*
> *that he can't remember making,*
> *that's been punished past the mark.*

4. JUST CRAZY THINKING

He didn't like being caged up.

        went into the bedroom, put a .30-caliber

He had a real deep-down-inside
meanness, just like my dad.

        boilermaker's helper, his emotions

I think it was just his coming up
through all those years, not having
any real person you could look up to
and trust and talk to and respect
what they say to you.

        his emotions in tatters, went into the bedroom

He was impulsive.

        Winchester rifle against his chest

He told me he was a burden
to me and my wife. I told him
that was just crazy thinking, you know,
my brother's keeper and that kind of thing.
He thought, with people having
to take care of him like that,

he was a bum, living with us.
Really, he wasn't.

      "Goodbye, trouble," said the note

I just laughed it off, you know.

                     Someone has hurt me

I told him that was just crazy thinking.

      A few days before, in a fit

He had a real deep-down-inside
meanness, just like my dad.

            in a fit of apparent rage he drew
            a hunting knife across the girlfriend's

I just laughed it off, you know.

            the girlfriend's name on his arm,
            cutting the flesh so deeply
            that he destroyed the letters of the tattoo

"I love you both very much
"so don't forget about me OK.

            and pulled the trigger

[77]

"I'm sorry if I scratched your gun
"and I'm sorry I had to use it

       put a .30-caliber Winchester rifle

"but it was all I could find for a week.

       against his chest and pulled the trigger

"I would like you to do me
"a favor I know you don't like her
"but for me. Tell her I love her
"very much. I love you all.

       When his brother

"Goodbye trouble."

       When his brother and sister-in-law
       returned, the television set
       and the lights were on

I don't think he understood what
he was doing, that it would be permanent.

I have a personal need in my life

lying on the edge of the bed
with both feet on the floor
the rifle between his legs

He was impulsive.

bullet hole in his chest

5. READ THIS

THIRST IN THE LORD WITH ALL YOUR HEART
     AND HE WILL ACKNOWLEDGE AND HE WILL LIGHT
     THE WAY.
THIS PRAYER HAS BEEN SENT TO YOU FOR LUCK:
IT HAS BEEN AROUND THE WORLD NINE TIMES.
THE LUCK HAS BEEN BROUGHT TO YOU.
YOU ARE TO RECEIVE GOOD LUCK, WITHIN FOUR DAYS
     OF RECEIVING THIS LETTER.
THIS IS NO JOKE YOU WILL RECEIVE IN THE MAIL.
SEND A COPY OF THIS LETTER TO PEOPLE YOU THINK
     NEED GOOD LUCK.
DO NOT SEND MONEY.
DO NOT KEEP THIS LETTER.
IT MUST LEAVE YOUR HANDS WITHIN NINETY-SIX HOURS
     AFTER YOU RECEIVE IT.

AN HFS OFFICER RECEIVED $90,000.
DON RILLIST RECEIVED $59,000 AND LOST IT
     BECAUSE HE BROKE THE CHAIN.
WHILE IN THE PHILLIPINES GENERAL VOLEN LOST HIS LIFE
     SIX DAYS AFTER RECEIVING THIS LETTER.
HE FAILED TO CIRCULATE THIS PRAYER.
HOWEVER BEFORE HIS DEATH HE RECEIVED $795,000.
PLEASE SEND TWENTY COPIES AND SEE WHAT HAPPENS TO YOU
     ON THE FOURTH DAY.
THE CHAIN COMES FROM VENEZUELA AND WAS WRITTEN

BY SOL ANTHONY DE CACIAF A MISSIONARY FROM
SOUTH AMERICA.

SINCE THIS CHAIN MUST MAKE A TOUR OF THE WORLD
YOU MUST MAKE TWENTY COPIES IDENTICAL
TO THIS ONE AND SEND IT TO YOUR FRIENDS
PEOPLE AND AXQUAINTANCIES.

AFTER A FEW DAYS YOU WILL GET A SURPRISE.

THIS AFTER, EVEN IF YOU ARE SUPERSTITIOUS.

TAKE NOTE CONTAIMO DIAZ RECEIVED THE CHAIN IN 1953
HE ASKED HIS SECRETARY TO MAKE TWENTY COPIES
AND SEND THEM, FEW DAYS LATER HE WON A LOTTERY
FOR 2 MILLION DOLLARS IN HIS COUNTRY.

CORL CRODULT AN OFFICE EMPLOYEE RECEIVED THE CHAIN
HE FORGOT IT AND IN A FEW DAYS HE LOST HIS JOB.
HE FOUND THE CHAIN AND SENT IT TO TWENTY PEOPLE.
FIVE DAYS LATER GOT AN EVEN BETTER JOB.

COLIN HOUCEILA RECEIVED THE CHAIN AND DOUBT BELIEVING
HE THREW IT AWAY, NINE DAYS LATER HE DIED.

DO NOT SEND MONEY
DO NOT BRAKE THE CHAIN.

6. SERMON OF THE NEW PREACHER

You will ask me, then, What *are* the things of the spirit. Even the fire on the hearth, I tell you, the morning light, and cleanliness, and gratitude, and the mother's love of her small child, and the pattern in the leaf or wing. . . . All things not material; as has been said.

That is why even the incarceration of some of you may be a spiritual experience, it will remove you from the material, I will hope, as much you as the monk who chooses it.

But without commandments and a new heart, neither confinement nor a show of goodness is anything more than a useless feeding of delicate fruits to the ravening bloodthirsty dog of your brute snarling, your unkindness, your meanness, your lack of feeling, your blindness!

You have committed the crimes and already you are caged and you do not know it!

But Brother, you say. Brother, I have needs, I'm in trouble, or I'm in pain, or I have sorrows and worries and wounds! I'm in debt, and my son won't straighten out, and my wife doesn't love me the way she once did, Brother, I'm talking about me!

But I'll tell you, when the flames have risen up roaring but a brief while through the dry wood, and died again, and the orange coals waver and glow under a small hot tongue of fire, that is the fire of the spirit.

When brick upon brick is piled until at the summit a great building ends and the air begins again, that is the air of the spirit.

When you look in the morning mirror, well-disposed to yourself, or at odds with yourself and striving against yourself as if you were an enemy to your own heart, and suddenly you see a spider retreat behind the mirror that you knew not had spun a web so brazenly in the household, to draw its web across your very face!—that is the spider of the spirit.

When after housework and day-labor you angrily taunt and torment each other you're so weary, and as you speak your shadows move across the cold wall which they do not touch or in any way change, that is the movement of the spirit.

And when the athlete's tired body sleeps and he dreams of his father, or she dreams of her mother, and weeps in the dream, that is the cleansing of the spirit.

I will not tell you some end of man is nigh, why do I need to tell you? We are each of us the end of man, the end of all men and women. And the beginning which is the beginning of the spirit.

I will make a list from A even unto Z of your wicked acts and your puny unavailing confessions and alibis, and I tell you the truth, I do not hold great hope for you.

You hop and dance from one thing to another and leave everything unfinished or done poorly. You wake in haste and you sleep in haste, you will even die in haste! Don't be surprised by it, or feel you weren't warned!

You have too many of everything and not enough of anything.

Your mind leaps off like a fly from what it should dwell upon and instead of quiet thought you want rowdy commerce and loud clamoring, you cannot get enough of it.

Do you think there will be another life for you in which to take your time and do everything over again properly? Do you think killing a weak little impulse of good that is struggling in you for life is no more than killing a fly?

You are in the air, I tell you, leaping over a chasm that is bottomless, even if to you it seems pretty narrow, it is far wider than you think.

You are like a mosquito that hovers against a confining window screen for hours because with its eyes smack against the fine mesh it cannot see the gaping hole above it through which it could easily pass.

You are like the leaf in autumn that, mistaking its fall for a moment's flight, thinks it will rise again when later it puts its mind to it.

Oh I could preach to you, but I won't any more.

I won't sharpen any more my pencils against you.

I won't any more close my door and sit down at my desk of wood.

I won't any more toil at the word.

I won't any more put on robes and climb the steps

to the pulpit, I won't any more raise my voice against you, or for you.

I won't any more wait for you at the door to clasp you as you leave.

I will take off my robes and retire into the world.

I will keep silent and use my hands for some good work.

When I see you I will turn my back to you.

I will reject your promises and apologies.

I will smash the dovecote and despoil the garden that I made for you.

I will not warn, I will judge.

I will not teach or console, I will punish.

Or so I say I will do. Do not test me, please, any further, brothers. Plead no more with me, sisters. I have said what I can say, and what I can do, I have done; no more can I add to either.

Let us say an amen, now, and go.

7. WITNESS

I had a funny feelin when the phone rang.
    "Dja hear me shootin?" my neighbor said.
    "No, Jim"—it's half a mile—"not a thang."
"Za big rattlesnake, uz in the shed,
       must be six feet if it's an eench,
        Ah got it with muh .22, one shot, come on
         fore the crowd."
"OK," I said, "But I'ze just about to peench
       off a loaf, then I'll be over."
       It's like when somethin bad is a cinch
    ta happen, an you feel like time's never
       goin to start up again,
       it makes you wanta run for cover,
    that's the way I felt when I sat down
       on the toilet for a minit or two.
       I'd have to go on ta his place an by then
    he'd of called everbody he knew
       an stopped traffic and something bad ud happen.
       An it did, too, cause this biker come through
    lookin for trouble, seem like, all bint
       outa shape cuzza this buncha people
       in the road blockin iz fast way for im
    an he got pissed off an beeped
       iz liddle horn an started pushin um back
       with'z bike till he looked up

an Jim uz holdin iz snake up high, it uz like
    somethin *happened* to im when he saw it,
    he went kinda crazy cuzza that snake,
an tried ta run down this kid
    who'z about ta cut the rattles off
    for Jim, an this biker barely hit
iz brakes an turned a liddle, just enough,
    an people are yellin at im, he's about *so*
    close ta catchin it, but he's actin tough,
he says, "I coulda hitcha if I'da wanted to, ya know,"
    "Yeah, you jist try it," Jim says, cause
    now he's picked up iz *shotgun*, it's always loaded,
this biker pulls out a pistol an blows
    the snake in two, layin there, an then points it at Jim,
    but that's his mistake. Because
you won't take another shot at *enny*thang
    if you don't hit whatcha want to first,
    an Jim already had iz gun up an bang
the guy went flyin off iz bike with'z chest
    shot away an hit the road dead an iz bike
    fell over an that was it, it happened so fast
you could still hear the shot, it uz like
    one a those thangs you do as a reflex
    without thinkin, you're psyched,
ya know? —An then ya think, God A-mighty, it's Texis,
    ya just shot and killed the guy
    an you're not sure now *what* to expect.

About a dozen widnessess'll all say
    it wadn't exactly your fault
    but they *seen* you do it in the lighta day.
You may be guilty even if you don't *feel* some guilt.
    Well here came the depitty sheriffs all at once
    from the county, an got Jim and everbody felt
awful when they put the biker's worthless body in the
    am-bu-lance
    an drove off leavin iz blood still on the road.
    That boy with the knife took the rattles, since
nobody else cared about em, an Jim's dog growled
    at me when I rolled the dead man's bike away
    into the shed where the *snake*'d been, my God,
    like iz life ud
keep goin and he'd be back for it some day,
    an I don't know what he died for,
    an I don't know why,
but it seemed like a thang that couldn't be helped, no more
    than it could've been foretold. They just ring
    in my head, both those shots, till I'm sore
with the sound of um, it uz a bad, wrong
    needless, wasteful thing, with no lesson in it,
but by now *somebody* on this road has wrote a song
    about it probly, it'll come on the radio in a minit.

8. THE SNARLING DOG
(A Song, Loud & Rough)

Brother, have you heard them speak
of the recent quarrel between two sisters
who tore at each other's hair and eyes
till both were blind and bald last week?
An awful crime, and which is to blame?
  Brother, I was there.

Did you know in the morning paper it said
that two city gangs have stormed and warred
through the streets all month, and both so scared
they couldn't quit to count the dead?
And for what kind of fame?
  Brother, I was there.

You heard, I guess, about the school
where the brute teachers terrorized
the children and tore their tiny prize
hearts out of childhood with threats to kill,
after sexual torment and acts of slime?
  Brother, I walked by that school unaware.

In this hospital nearby—did you already hear?—
they've got a case of two little boys
dying of burns all over their bodies
who painted themselves and then caught fire.

Where was their mother and dad at the time?
    Brother, I wish I'd been there.

In some other country we sent our soldiers to
the place blew up and one young man
waited holding just a hand in the ruin
till finally it clawed his and went limp and let go!
(He himself suffered wounds and is lame.)
    Brother, they shouldn't've been there.

    That's what it's come to, we're told,
    behind the playground gate there's a snarling dog,
    he's everywhere, he leaps at your leg
    and gets it and won't let loose his hold.

    The snarling dog is in your locked car.
    The snarling dog's in your medicine chest.
    He'll tear at the hand you make a fist
    then he'll jump out again from your nightstand drawer.

    He can spring full size from a crack or a crumb.
    From the pages of your book he'll attack on sight.
    He's waiting in the garage shadows at night.
    When the TV picture comes on, it's him.

    An old lost lady will look frail and slight—
    it's the snarling dog dressed in her rags.
    You hand your money to the checker for your bags
    and the dog will thrash out of one and bite.

The snarling dog is in bedrooms and halls,
it walks the roads from dark till dawn,
then it gets up again and goes on,
slavering through barracks and ballfields and schools.

He breaks in at night leading thieves and assassins
and raves through the house, mauling the children.
He attacks funerals, and puts cold dread in
everyone by leaping up onto the coffins.

Brother, I've seen him and I've come to warn
because he's on my trail, not a minute behind.
You'll see, believe me—you too will find
you're running to pass the warning on.

Have you heard people tell of the danger to us all
when this one's elected or that one breaks jail?
It's twice what you heard anyone tell
and they got the snarling dog on a chain at heel.

9. CASH OR TURTLE OR HEAVEN

Just beyond that big sign for Ebenezer Church?—
you know the one—and Ellsworth's Polled Herefords?—
I had to swerve to miss a turtle in the lane
and I looked in the rearview and I saw the pickup
behind me, that was loaded too high anyway
with old furniture and all, swerve in order to
hit the damn thing, and I hope it set
the sonofabitch back about five lifetimes.
Lindy sitting next to me, all she could
talk about was getting new sunglasses, like mine,
said she wanted the Zodiac ones, though,
so she could personally express herself, *her* sign.
What about you? Do any camping? Like to fish?
I just can't get away much these days, I'm short of cash.

*

The boss knows what's best for you, you don't
have to ask him for anything, he already
knows what you need, so every morning you should
hunch over your coffee and say this prayer:
Our father, which art
in business, incorporated be thy name.
Thy profit come, thy will be done,
at work as it is in Congress.
Give us this day our daily wage.
And extend our credit, as we have had
to give you those benefit concessions.
And lead us not into grievances or strikes,

but deliver us from unions: for thine
is the profit, and the power, and the lobby forever. Amen.

*

But I never will have all the cash I need.
That's a hell of a thing, that turtle, isn't it?
I hit a goddamn deer once, it broke
the windshield and smashed the fender in
like it was tinfoil—surprise you—I had it made
into sausage, though, and we ate that
for a whole winter. That was even before
I lost my job. Could use the meat now,
even getting it that way. And before Lindy
started going back to church with the kids.
I don't like to go much, I wasn't raised to it
like she was, don't see the point. If there is
a heaven, they got to keep some of these
goddamned bastards out of there, I say and believe.

10. IN THE VIOLENT WARD

Like patients walking down
a windowed corridor sunlit from one side,
through trapezoids of light
through the cold bars of shade,

we can't be sure we want to get well—
once you go out, time starts again
your wounds may heal
and you'll want to wound someone.

All violent people secretly desire
to be curbed by something that they respect.
It can be the law, or their own children,
or the zodiac. It can be an ice pick.

It's so they may become known
to themselves. (But none of us
is known to another, we can't be.)
And not to be more like brutes but less.

And when not curbed, turning lethal and mad
they may rage till the last little bit
of anger is drowned, then they're mild
with the blood, they're pure, they're quiet.

But they'll hurt you still, you hear?
Stay away from them, they're bad.

They're waiting for some glorious mistaken expected one
and if you're not him you're dead.

They're waiting for what it is
that they'll respect, but they can't imagine
what it will be, they're afraid to know.
And till it comes to them, gentle or mean,

they'll still be sick or wounded,
afflicted somehow to be put in here
in these hallways and rooms, edgy with
this stale whispering we do, in this drugged air.

I mean with us: here where we all
spend our days walking, unfit,
wondering who among us may put steel
into another; who holds the whip; who needs to feel it.

The National Poetry Series 1985

Stephen Dunn
Local Time
selected by Dave Smith

Alice Fulton
Palladium
selected by Mark Strand

Reginald Gibbons
Saints
selected by Roland Flint

Jack Myers
As Long As You're Happy
selected by Seamus Heaney

Lynn Doyle
Living Gloves
selected by Cynthia McDonald

The National Poetry Series was established in 1978 to publish five collections of poetry annually through five participating publishers. The manuscripts are selected by five poets of national reputation. Publication is funded by James A. Michener, Edward J. Piszek, The Ford Foundation, The Witter Bynner Foundation, and the five publishers—E.P. Dutton, Graywolf Press, Persea Books, University of Illinois Press, and William Morrow & Co.